THE SLIP

THE SLIP

GEORGE TYSH

BLAZEVOX[BOOKS]
Buffalo, New York

THE SLIP
by George Tysh
Copyright © 2015

Published by BlazeVOX [books]

Printed in the United States of America

Interior design and typesetting by Geoffrey Gatza
Cover and interior art by Janet Hamrick

First Edition
ISBN: 978-1-60964-217-4
Library of Congress Control Number: 2015937798

BlazeVOX [books]
131 Euclid Ave
Kenmore, NY 14217

Editor@blazevox.org

publisher of weird little books

BlazeVOX [books]

blazevox.org

21 20 19 18 17 16 15 14 13 12 01 02 03 04 05 06 07 08 09 10

BlazeVOX

ALSO BY GEORGE TYSH

SIT UP STRAIGHT

CHEAPNESS MEANS FORGIVENESS

MECANORGANE

SHOP/POSH

TEA

OVALS

ECHOLALIA

DREAM SITES

THE IMPERFECT

"In his fall he understood that he was heavier
than his dream and he loved, from then on,
the weight that had made him fall."

— Pierre Reverdy

Table of Contents

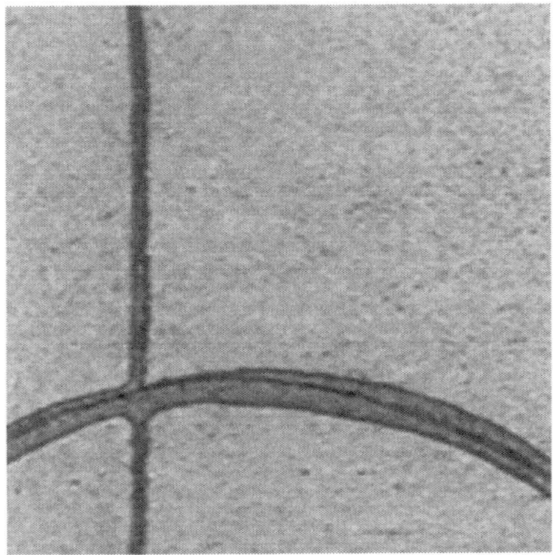

I

The Slip

The Slip

sometimes

    set or whole

        a quiet fear

           wears

    sleeves of death

dancers *au pair*

    a piano

        sounding

          the song

    we wish to hear

"All Mysteries"

    rumbles

        in evening air

          of rain tracing

    snow trails

to

    which we turn

        and ringing

          interrupts the dance

"the separation

of movement from

steady rhythm"

an embryo

from an impresario

plowing

salting

and then no matter

"far from breaking

up the whole,

false

continuities are"

still there

a quiet fear

wearing sleeves

of death's

elegance

après tout

2.

open palm

        above the cup

              emanate waves

                     of oolong

peripheral

       glimpse of wool

             cap as letters

                    arrive

resisting the

      impulse to move from a

             state of lesser

                  to greater complexity

accidentally

      a leg posed

           on this narrow

                plane of sun

we (incomprehend)

      in the space

          between words

              tracing

                  steps

3.

pursuit and capture

                confinement
                        and restraint
                                the pleasures of the spirit

are inexhaustible:
              — to be stolen
                        from a room at
                              night

and taken to a
             faraway land

                    — to be held down
                            somewhere

what love
        that has such people
                  if we have it to explain
                          the surprise

is "dutiful"
        as it drifts into
                further
                    reaches
                        unspoken

4.

> quiet rains
>> over nothing
>>> and back to
>>>> solace
> save the mode
>> water
>>> falling on iron hills

> a dragon sips
>> welcome peace
>>> its icon arranged

> on the bottle
>> a product
>>> of a particular
>>>> malady

> that thus
>> one may fear
>>> the throes of
>>>> a "moist sweet"

> muffled by clothes
>> or a distinct
>>> teardrop

> in underbrush
>> a hailstorm
>>> through brambles

> the sighing of
>> a penis
>>> in some forgotten
>>>> hell

5.

what is it
   of the untried
      American
        partner

that would lead
   "at this evening
      hour" to unseemly
        delight

"I will leave
   you by yourself
     white dream," it
       seemed to say

the words were
   hardly out of
     place in our
       murmuring

and "shut the
   closet to conceal
     the strange, wraithlike
       apparel it contained"

who would believe
   now, I thought"
     these wrappings
       this incessant

rain
  of longing
    and stirring

6.

"stepping forth"

        (an angel

            on a sidewalk)

                  from clouds

the not-

      yet-scandal

          of the thing

                shown

its *gai savoir*

      of

         specters in heels

                thrown

into illicit

     becoming

        as they undo the

             "specimen dream"

7.

the top of his head
                    flies off
                              in response to some screams

it matters not
              that she
                        inflates a divan

with every breath
                  their storm
                              widens across the tranquil
                                                          earth
the heart throbs
                before the
                          screen goes dark

under formal eaves a fan
                        turns slowly
                                    to bubbling brooks of laughter

what is it
          that she
                  now knows more?

"or perhaps she rules through
                            the beauty
                                      you sometimes mention"
                                                            at night

8.

abstraction
   soaked
      in vinegar
         23 seconds

smoking weeds
    of an illusion
       rising with the sun
          in showers

there is no
   doubt
     and floods
       the heart

9.

"sophisticated women"
                    brush
                              unthinkable hair

and stare
              wildly at calamity
                              as if playing with moss

"illusions are
              more common than changes
                                        in fortune"

says the lady
              who "would stop you
                              as you went by"

and "continue painting
                    after the end of
                              painting" pink

lips and toes

Nothing by You

strange brew
                  smoky surface
                        and mahogany
                              depths

                  your
                        love-lone-liness
                              after midnight

to hear it
            in my sleep

"We move with ease

                  from one to the other"

                              nothing by you

                  omitted without discomfort

that aerosol
in the face of
thought

                  (precisely
                        what occasions)

                        a persistent odor
                  of whatever you like
                              between women

this our doing

                  as night falls
            into night
                              out
                  of
sleep

                  (gender, *femmes*, "race," etc.)

building casts a partial

shadow

there are cars and sun

evidence of ignorance

hooks in stays

a voice in darkness calling

id to idiot
wanter to wanker

to my place
at the
farther wall

(*modéré*)

noble
sentimental
supple
elemental

practiced
joy

"Along the way

our lives...

repeatedly

changed"

L'Avventura

        infinite works and days

            (love of paranoia)

                with their

furtive pleasures

            but icy and tingling

       "the moon stood still"

(in)visible shining hand

            sketches

        4 a.m.
        mist

Circled

murmurs

dans la cour

you suppose

halfway

to the dream

a
second
quartet's

intervals

a
fourth
movement's

largesse

the opiate

shared

Once

    the femme

        puts on

            nylon(s)

                & continues

            for many

        men and

  years

  thus moving

        from repose

            to response

                in a direct

            discrete

        relation

"how came it about?"

you ask

     beginning

         simply

            and going on

Fork

"I rode

              without

                              seeing the way"

well nigh

              the

                              exit of time

              its

pas de deux

              lost

                      and remembered

o belle fleur

          after night

                          is gone

Married

       to the muse

                of contemplation

                          a little bit ago

                          "The dream was

                breaking my bones..."

      bowered

            carrefour

                    of the Quartier

                            Latin

                  shadowy

           beckoning

    leaves

        their entrails

               among

                    throngs & flâneurs

"Desire

is the other things,

in great number."

"Color is fooling

us all

the time."

and thus there are

in their endless

usages

words

to be uncovered

a yearning to

"release me"

(again)

It was the quietest

August morning ever,

with just some tiny

cicada engines

running in the weeds

Dream

drama-

mine

uncon-

vertible

una-

voidable

darkening

transitional

object

in

potential

space

like talking

with

difficulty

like art,

useless

not

irrelevant

childhood shoes

in branches of

silver

maple

"I decide

what I am

going to do

from a distance"

reset date

and time

"two

places

at

once"

oranges

de Californie,

blue-veined

trellis of

an afterthought,

"my

bowl of

nothing"

in your eyes

untied

"Everything

    ...played out

        in this double

           relationship"

           pervert-plaintiff

        not plenitude

    submissive-substitute

not subordinate

as it breaks loose

    from bonds

        and loosens the bindings

          of volumes

          noiselessly alive

        an orgy of

    whispers

at the top of her voice

acoustic record

    scratched

        and materially indifferent

          to her complaint

from the family

    in exile

          stars over landfill

            moon over town

tolling of bells

    covered by clouds

        "the existence

          of a mass

strand

    of workers

        at once

          attached

to the idea

    of self-

        emancipation

          and hostile

to" repose

    after toil &

        other forms

          of erasure

incipient heartbreak

                ignores the plan

                            rosebuds

                                    block entrances

                            and exits

                igniting

"the power of falsity"

                in the country

                          "There is a world

                                  underneath"

                                mister man

                        and she "loved,

                from then on,

the weight"

mascara running

                (ithyphallic)

                          in summer downpour

                                    a bath

                          while

                making

art

defined by

      whalebone

            "the silence of

                  doors and

                  windows
            and the quivering

      voice
of the light"

      calling up from

            depths

                  where
            boulevards

      intersect
with mise-en-scène

      ultraviolet

            priapus

                  one morning

            quaffs a potion

      halfway to
dawn

seamless

       brûlée

               "the

                    telephone

               rings,

       all

is

       lost"

               my

                    head

               of

       rhymes

your

       cadence

               your

                    response

                    a

               love

       beyond

measure

La Notte

                                                 "fringed

                          by a light

          from far away"

                         swollen

                                              river in fog

"o great wall
     of sadness

                  blotting out
                      the sky"

                                      today, tonight

                         there is

              less of it

in batches

                quelle surprise!

                                        s/he's lithe

                        in the loafers

              with huge

poufy hair

                  (may the eyes
                     say "yes")

"o great wall
     of sunlessness

                    blot out
                      the (im)perfect"

                                      nothing but
                                        whiteness

                        (window

          opens within)

as when a piece

                    takes its place

                                        the peace

                    that comes

with knowing

                "is not one"

mon mari!

changes and makes

of me

a sight

as if written

for editing

blackened &

blued

to break the

constrictures

thus devised

("seeing without having")

a boy-child

swathed

in surgical vestments

of the femme-trance

devours its perfume

*   *   *

lavender suds   cover over

the same thing

                                                      the same time

                        comes another

overcome by

                          pursed lips

                                                3 a.m.

                    you'll know me

                                        not

"in absence

                        finds the only

                                                    possibility..."
"oh"

                        in snow

                                                on a roof

"my"

                    a sigh

                                    on the floor

                                                        beneath

  nebulous

                    moonrise

                                    bare

                                                mummery

                        sky's

            "final

                        ceiling"

                        *   *   *

bluebells ring

      are

          you listening?

adjusted to a

      narrow

         line of streets

in doors

      dank

         dark hallways

may know

     (*mais non*)

        a slip

          of the tongue

in lips

     a surplus

       of endurance

           to enfold

       (not the business

    of the world

unfurled)

       this curtain of

          blue

II

Sexistential

caring
& daring

undress
w/ *tendresse*

linger
to finger

"wet-
in-wet"

one
gone

birches
as bitches

to me
a tome

in memory
not theory

in anger
at the danger

to her
heart

under a pine
we pine

family
ruins multiply

what will
allow

me to sit
apart

unsettled
nay, rattled

shine
on, line

safe
from surf's

thunder
of despair

plunder-
ful hair

our mouths
gone south

self
onto shelf

crumble
then tumble

a moment
of torment

"The sluts
flit"

"the world
becoming world"

some
one

"toing
and froing"

from morality
to mortality

adrift
in mist

"the pose,
the poise"

Those

           opulent

           rains

    "areas of

           dark

                human consent"

           stalks

           and

           blooms

boule-

ver-

sement

du

rapport

rien

et

là

se

laisse

lire

such

antennas

know the

voice

of undoing

long

before we

"If you do
I'll keep you"

gesture
of a lamp

from
depths

(murmuring
chorus)

that we
recognize

own sake
at stake

*

the at
long last

tedious
disguise

taken to
extremes

"by his lightest
touch"

the slightest
tincture

used
unused

*

plus-signs
above the clouds

"sounds
that work"

in the still
born night

signs
lost in clouds

steeped in
ancient

reams
abandoned

On the Rim

the bleached
asshole

of morality
says

not for you
this love

of leaving
papa pain

there is only
a spotlight

where your head
used to happen

it's witchcraft
mama!

"the life that we
loved was elsewhere"

accentuated
attenuated and

abbreviated
as the Buddha said

(ailanthus blossoms)

III

Unrealism

"Each word alone with the other"
                    — Laura Moriarty

sun
sinking
low
onto

second
story
door-
way

impassive
inert
locked
in

long
moments
of
dark

*

during
the
whole
of

what
they
led
to

*fait
accompli,*
a
torch

carried
around
thru
time

*

a
thing
borne
along

each
object
reflecting
the

beauty
of
the
sunset

but
away
from
it

*

our
bodies
so
similar

where
a
thing
ends

a
thousand
waters
and

the
deep
and
dank

a
steeple
bell
tolls

the
hour
of
your

be-
lovèd
symp-
tom

some
green
in
there

*

our
bodies
so
similar

(one
cock
under
God

in-
divi-
si-
ble)

and
begin
to
meld

As

                            little
                            as
                            impossible

Slip

        couilles
        à l'air

        lunes
        de miel

        au raz de
        mariée

arms
out
palms
turned

she
lifted
the
hair

that
shook
a
little

contorted
image
transformed
head

Dressed up

one
can
become
someone

a
metonym
for
either

the
costume
or
identity

there
is
no
solace

the
crave
the
craze

a
daze
of
days

the
ways
it
weighs

the
plays
it
plays

a
feeling
of
fleeing

a
poison
to
prison

and
the
wider
shores

in
a
last
tango

the
way
they
were

for
the
short
term

and
the
low
ceiling

but
not
for
us

*

at
the
last
minute

the
gray
area
between

and
more
than
mere

are
joined
together
here

an
early
ear
rises

to
subtle
hardly
audible

roaring
of
the
earth

le
plein
le
vide

*

pole
rhymes
with
stool

a
rebus
for
abuse

but
not
so
much

we're
only
here
briefly

*

this
dumb
engorged
flesh

as
on
a
scale

from
one
to
ten

lyrical
abject
unto
ideality

*

many
cries
for
water

in
the
hysteria
cafeteria

stainless
steel
and
enamel

eyebrow
worry
bye-bye
baby

a
hot
little
war

hurt
hurt
spurt
spurt

dirty
is
as
does

rip
off
those
unmentionables

joy
of
a
jet

lips
lids
and
lashes

infanta
of
the
pavane

in
koda-
chrome
sunset

Lo,

            the
            most

            lovely
            voice

            of
            all

            was
            the

            voice
            of

            the
            ass

(refrain) "Desire

is
the
other
things,

in
great
number."
"Color

is
fooling
us
all

the
time."
and
thus

there
are
in
their

endless
usages
words
to

be
uncovered
a
yearning

to
"release
me"
(again)

it
was
the
quietest

August
morning
ever,
with

just
some
tiny
cicada

engines
running
in
the weeds

nous,
les
morts

to
the
past

im-
perfect
world

from
our
human

tangle
of
legs

in
endless
bed

con-
fused
passion

in
con-
text

nous,
les
mots

NOTES

epigraph from Pierre Reverdy, *Prose Poems*, translated by Ron Padgett,
Brooklyn, New York: Black Square Editions, 2007

The Slip #1: Gilles Deleuze, *Cinema 1: The Movement-Image*, translated by
Hugh Tomlinson and Barbara Habberjam, Minneapolis:
University of Minnesota Press, 1986

#4: after Okakura Kakuzo, *The Book of Tea*, New York: Dover, 1964

#5: Charlotte Brontë, *Jane Eyre*, New York: Bedford/St. Martin's, 1996

#6: Kaja Silverman, *World Spectators*, Stanford: Stanford University Press, 2000

#7: Franz Kafka, *The Castle*, translated by Mark Harman, New York: Schocken
Books, 1998

#9: ARTFORUM: Summer 2011; and Franz Kafka, *The Castle*

Nothing by You: Gilles Deleuze, *Cinema 1: The Movement-Image*

L'Avventura: Fats Domino, "Blueberry Hill," Imperial, 1956

Once: Laura Riding, *Progress of Stories*, New York: Persea Books, 1994

Fork: Isaac Babel, *Collected Stories*, translated by David McDuff, London:
Penguin Books, 1994

Married: Isaac Babel, *Collected Stories*

"Desire: Laura Riding, *Progress of Stories*; and Josef Albers

Dream: Siri Hustvedt, *Living, Thinking, Looking*, New York: Picador, 2012; and
Kylee Weiss, unpublished poem

In the Country: Jacques Rancière, *Althusser's Lesson*, translated by
Emiliano Battista, London: Continuum, 2011;
Robert Creeley, "There..."; Maurice Maeterlinck and
Jean Epstein in Jacques Rancière, *Film Fables*, translated by
Emiliano Battista, Oxford: Berg, 2006

La Notte: Fernando Pessoa, *The Book of Disquiet*, translated by Richard Zenith,
London: Penguin Books, 2001; Luce Irigaray, *This Sex Which is Not One*,
translated by Catherine Porter, Ithaca: Cornell University Press, 1985

Ciel: Marek Bieńczyk, *Transparency*, translated by Benjamin Paloff, Champaign:
Dalkey Archive Press, 2012; Georges Poulet in Bieńczyk, *Transparency*;
Jack Spicer, *My Vocabulary Did This to Me: The Collected Poems of Jack
Spicer*, Middletown, Connecticut: Wesleyan University Press, 2008

Sexistential: Alex Danchev, *Cézanne: A Life*, New York: Pantheon Books, 2012

Those: Patti Smith, *Just Kids*, New York: Ecco, 2010

L'Eclisse: Emily Brontë, *Wuthering Heights*, Boston: Bedford/St. Martin's, 1992;
Henry James, *The Golden Bowl*, London: Penguin Books, 2009;
Keith Richards, *Life*, New York: Back Bay Books, 2010

On the Rim: Anne Wiazemsky, *Une Année Studieuse*, Paris: Éditions Gallimard, 2012
(my translation)

Unrealism epigraph from Laura Moriarty, *A Tonalist*, Callicoon, NY: Nightboat
Books, 2010

Mise-en-scène: part 2, Edgar Allan Poe, "The Fall of the House of Usher"
John Yau, *A Thing Among Things: The Art of Jasper
Johns*, New York: Distributed Art Publishers, 2008
part 3, Yau, *A Thing Among Things*
part 4, Yau, *A Thing Among Things*
Poe, "The Fall of the House of Usher"

L'Âge d'or: part 2, Yau, *A Thing Among Things*

Enfant terrible: Renee Gladman, *Event Factory*, Urbana, IL: Dorothy, 2010
    Yau, *A Thing Among Things*

Dressed Up: Yau, *A Thing Among Things*

Hand-in-hand: Adam Gopnik, "Word Magic," The New Yorker, May 26, 2014
    David Perlmutter, *Grain Brain*, New York: Little, Brown and
    Company, 2013

Ash: *Michael E. Smith catalogue*, Ludwig Forum Aachen, 2013
    (Brigitte Franzen, Anna Sophia Schultz, Simone Menegoi,
    Chris Sharp/Franz Kafka, Alexander Koch)

Crosswords: part 2, Brian O'Doherty, *Inside the White Cube: The Ideology of
    the Gallery Space* (Expanded Edition), Berkeley:
    University of California Press, 2000
    Spike Jonze, *her*, Annapurna Films, 2013
  part 3, Taylor Brady and Rob Halpern, *Snow Sensitive Skin*,
    Boston/Chicago/Olympia: Displaced Press, 2011
    *One Foot Out the Door: The Collected Stories of Lewis
    Warsh*, New York: Spuyten Duyvil Publishing, 2014

Unreason: Lesley Brill, *The Hitchcock Romance: Love and Irony in Hitchcock's Films*,
    Princeton: Princeton University Press, 1988

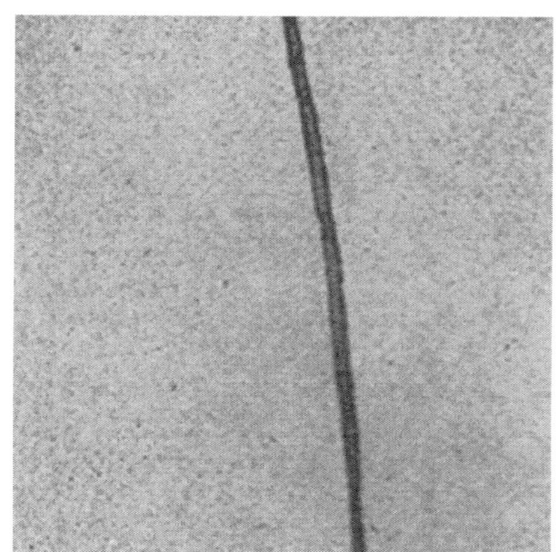

In Paris in the '60s, George Tysh edited the journal *Blue Pig* with poet David Ball, and collaborated with conceptual artists Christian Boltanski and Sarkis. From 1980 to 1991, he directed LINES: New Writing at the Detroit Institute of Arts, and (with poet Chris Tysh) edited In Camera, a project devoted to works of the sexual imaginary. He teaches film studies and poetics at the College for Creative Studies, Detroit. He is the recipient of a 2015 Kresge Artist Fellowship.

Janet Hamrick is a Detroit painter and printmaker, with work featured at jhamrick.com. Her calligraphic drawings grace Tysh's previous project, *The Imperfect* (United Artists Books, 2010).

Made in the USA
Monee, IL
07 July 2026